# PLAYWAY to English

**Second edition**

**1**

**Pupil's Book**

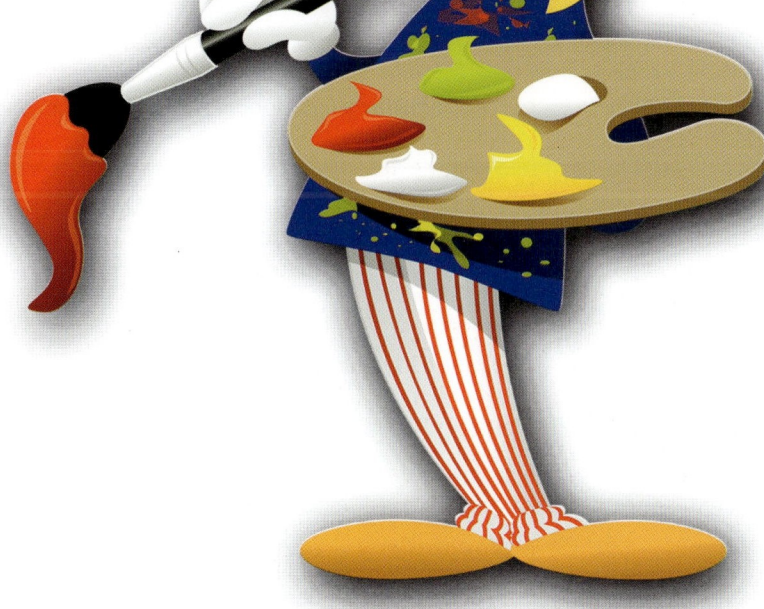

**Günter Gerngross • Herbert Puchta**

# Contents

## Unit 1: Hello     4–9

**Structures**
Good morning.
What's your name?
Hello, I'm Max/Benny/Linda/…
What is it?
Give me (yellow).
Here you are.
Yeah, all right.
A (red) bike/boat for (Linda).

**Vocabulary**
one, two, three, four
right, left
yes, no
red, yellow, green, blue, black, white
bike, boat
Stand up. Stretch. Shout 'Hooray!'.
Sit down.

## Unit 2: School     10–15

**Structures**
The (pencil) and the (glue), please.
Thank you.
Put your (pencil case) in your schoolbag.
It's not good/very good.
I'm sorry.
That's OK.

**Vocabulary**
five, six
schoolbag, pencil, pencil case,
scissors, glue, book, baby face
Close your eyes. Touch your nose.
Open your eyes. Listen. Smile.
pink, purple, orange

## Units 1–2: Show what you can do     16–17

## Unit 3: Fruit     18–23

**Structures**
What is it?
(Two) apples.
Give me more!
No way!
I'm thirsty.
I'm hungry.
Just a moment.
Help!

**Vocabulary**
apple(s), banana(s), plum(s), pear(s)

## Unit 4: Pets     24–29

**Structures**
What's this?
Let's play!
No, go away!
The mouse is (very) sad.

**Vocabulary**
cat, dog, hamster, mouse, duck, rabbit

## Units 3–4: Show what you can do     30–31

## Unit 5: Toys     32–37

**Structures**
My (blue) (train).
I've got (one) (car).
There's a (dog).

**Vocabulary**
seven, eight
teddy bear, train, plane, car, doll,
computer game, ball, puzzle, star
listen

## Unit 6: Weather — 38–43

**Structures** What's the weather like today? It's raining/snowing/sunny/windy/cloudy. What a sweet smell!

**Vocabulary** rain, sun, wind, clouds, snow
snowman, grow, run
bee, butterfly, a little seed, flower

## Units 5–6: Show what you can do — 44–45

## Unit 7: Party — 46–51

**Structures** A party for a (princess).
A (ghost) into a (sheriff).
Look at me!
You're a (magician).
Get a (piece of cake).

**Vocabulary** nine, ten
sheriff, princess, bear,
clown, crocodile, ghost, frog,
monster, magician, prince, bird

## Unit 8: Health — 52–57

**Structures** Have a (glass of milk).
(Three) (lollies), please.
What's the matter?
I feel sick.

**Vocabulary** Get out of bed. Wash your face.
Clean your teeth. Bend your knees.
Jump. Keep fit.
lemon, orange, chocolate, ice cream

## Units 7–8: Show what you can do — 58–59

## Unit 9: Food — 60–65

**Structures** Lots of …
(Chicken) is great.
I like …

**Vocabulary** butter, spaghetti, chicken, cheese, chips, ketchup, cornflakes, milk
spider
kitchen

## Unit 10: Animals — 66–71

**Structures** (The lion) is ill.
Stop it, please!

**Vocabulary** lion, elephant, monkey, snake, hippo
turtle, whale, mice, penguin

## Units 9–10: Show what you can do — 72–73

## Picture Dictionary — 74–79

**1**   Watch the story. Listen and stick.

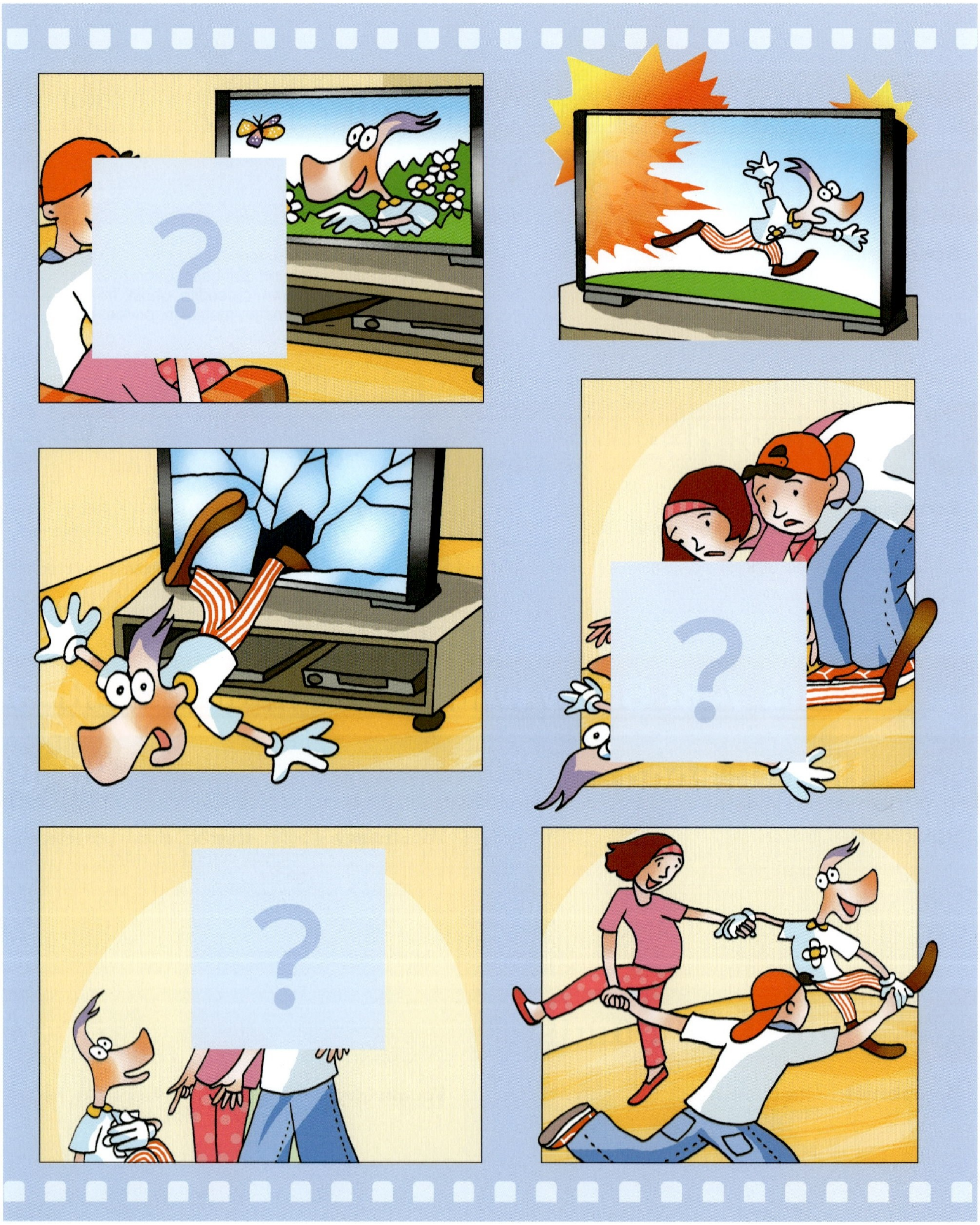

**2**  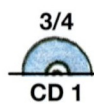 Sing the song.

Good morning.   What's your name?   Hello, I'm Benny/Max/Linda.

**3**  **Listen and point. Write the numbers.**

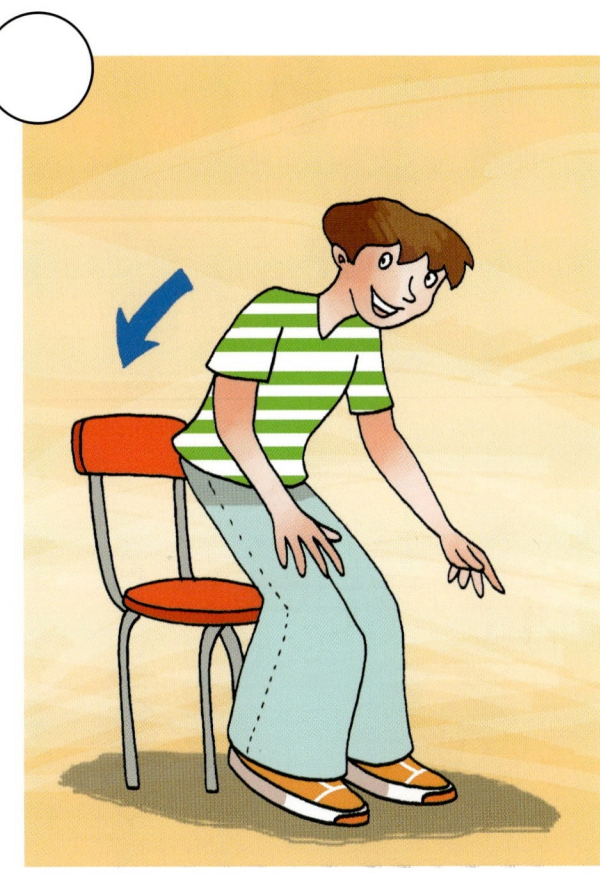
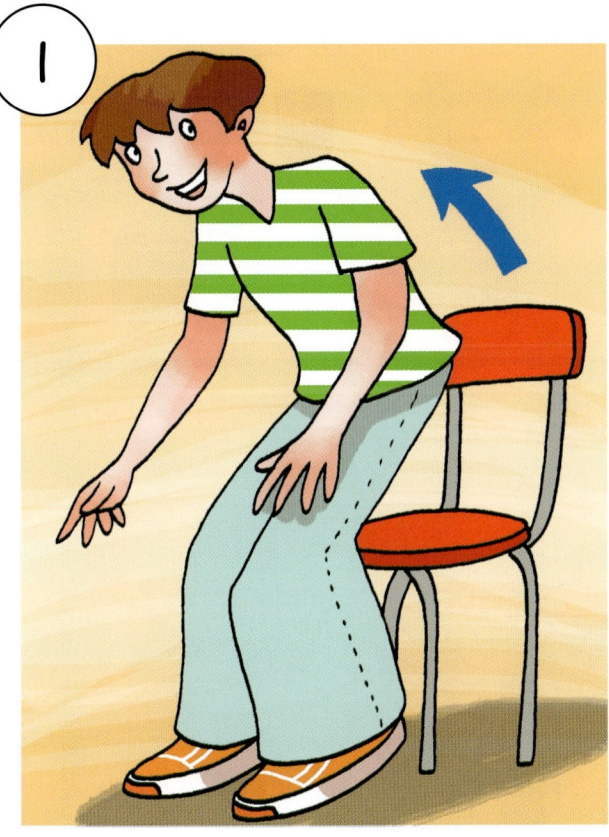

one   two   three   four   Stand up.   Stretch.   Shout 'Hooray!'.   Sit down.

# Unit 1

**4**  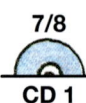 **Listen and point. Say the chant.**

Give me (red).   Here you are.

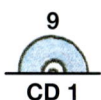 **Listen and point.**

  **Look and say.**

blue   white   red   black   green   brown   yellow

# Unit 1

**7**  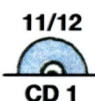 **Listen and colour. Say.**

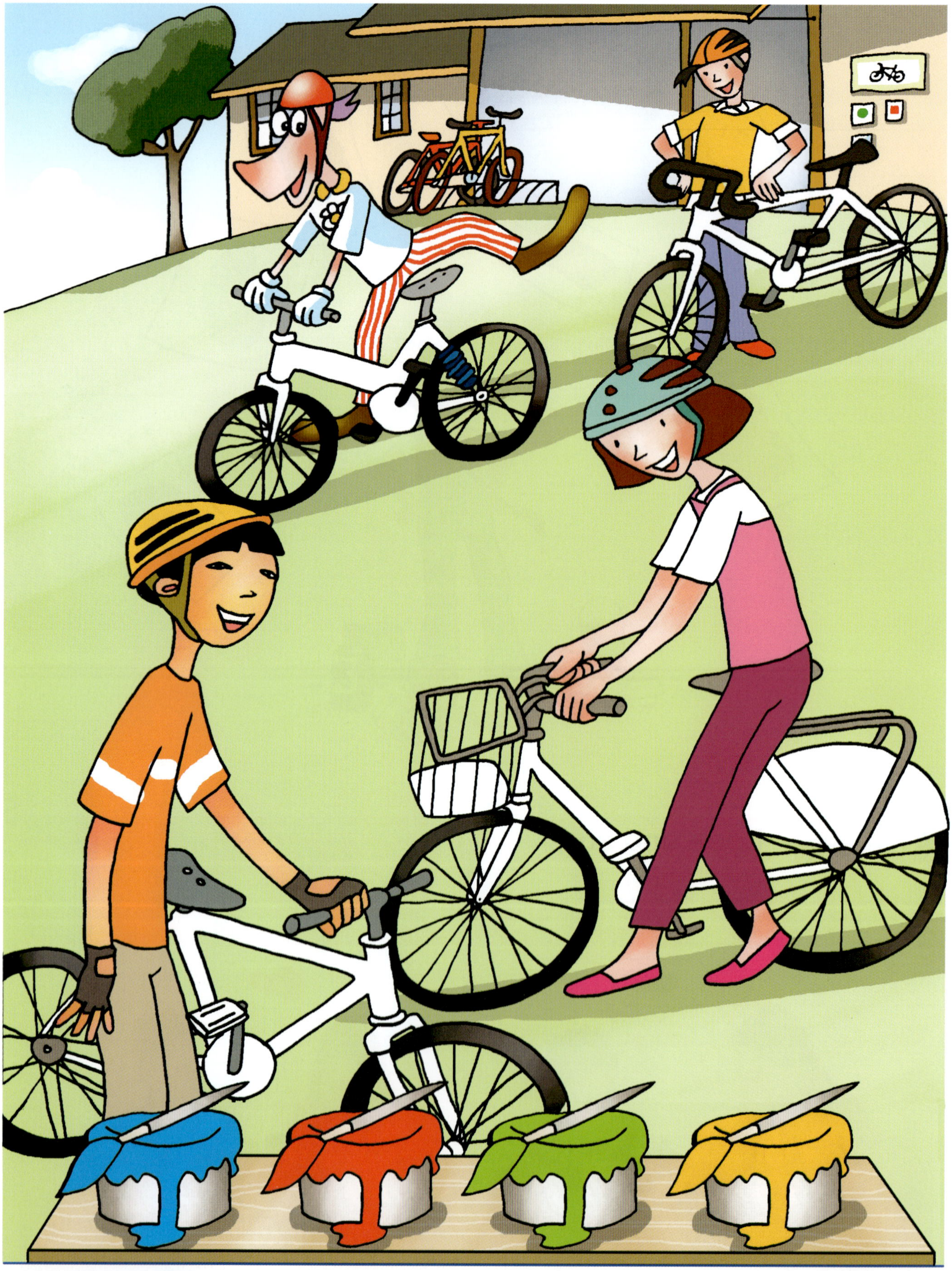

A (yellow) bike for (Benny).

**8** **Colour and say.**

A (blue) boat for (Max).

# Unit 2 School

**1** Listen and point. Say the chant.

schoolbag   pencil   pencil case   scissors   glue   book   baby face

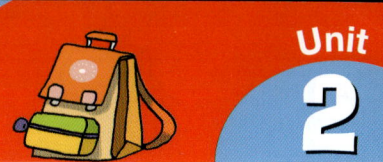

## 2 Listen and tick (✓).

18 CD 1

1

✓

2

3

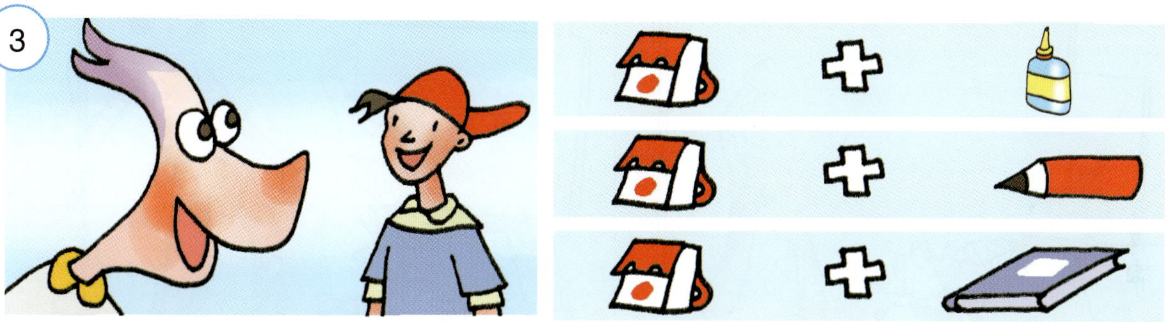

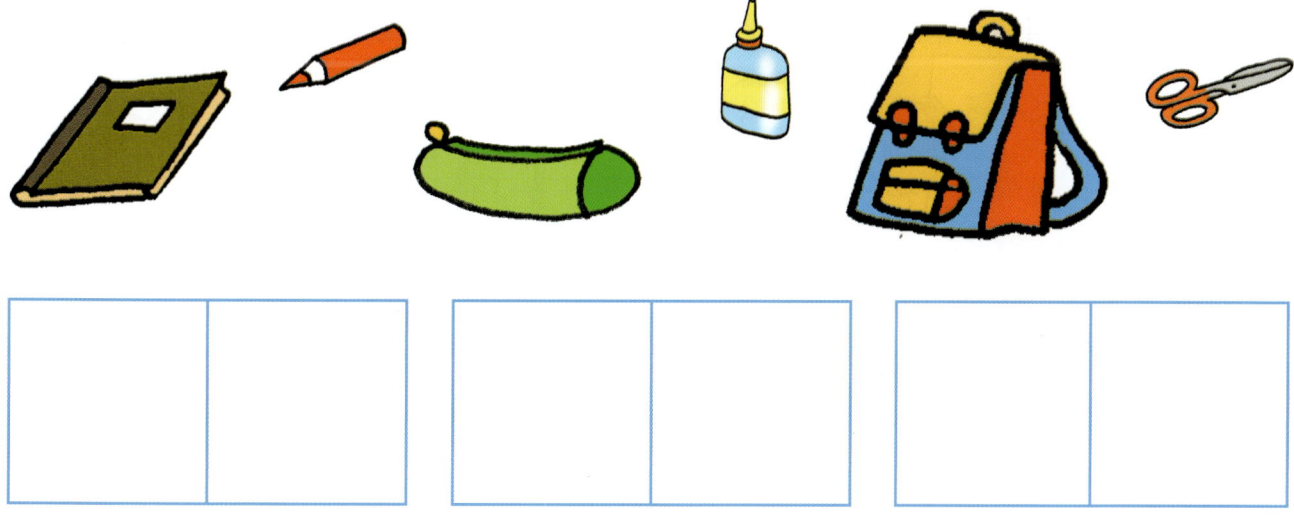

## 3 Stick and say.

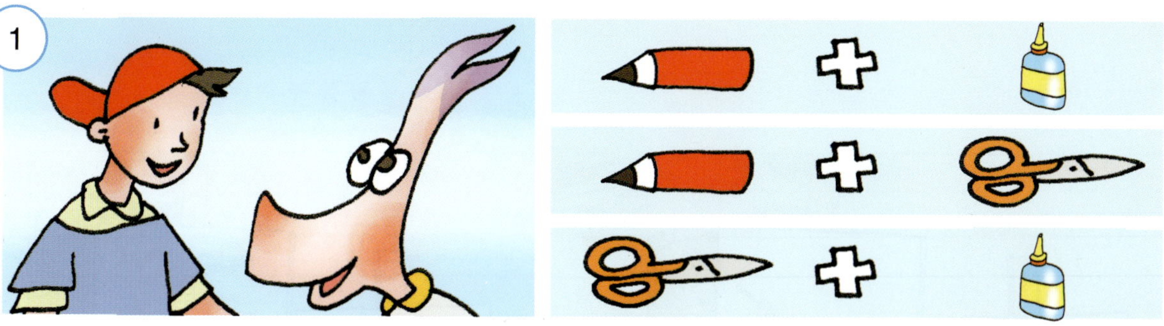

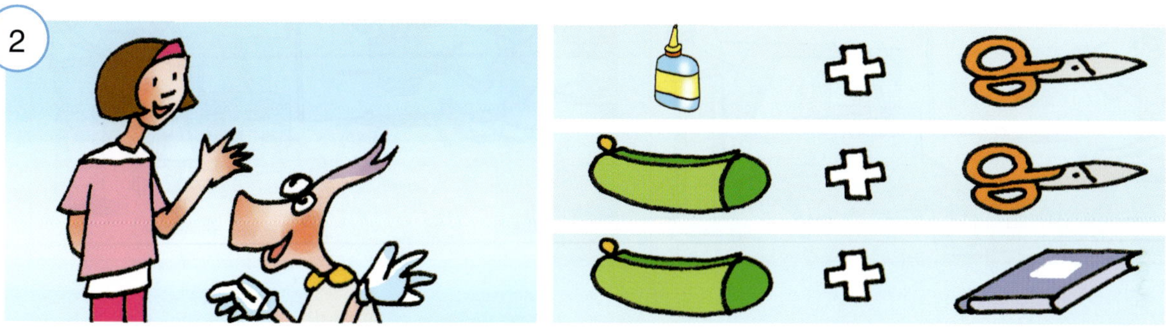

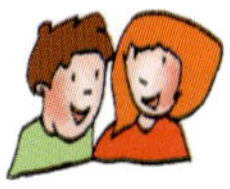

The (pencil) and the (glue), please. Thank you.

Unit 2

4   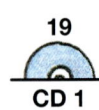 Watch the story. Listen and stick.

It's not good/very good.   I'm sorry.   That's OK.   I hate it.

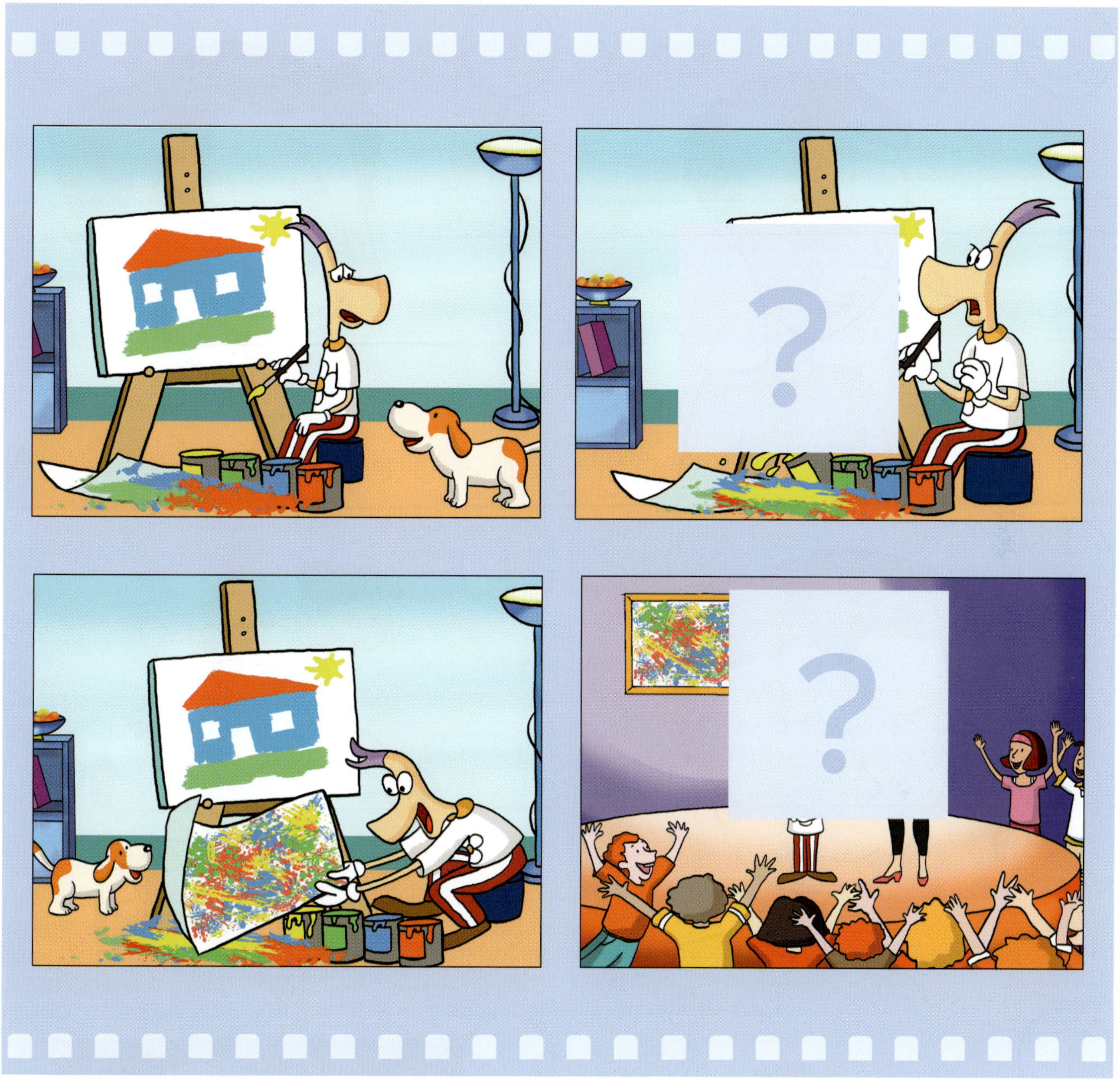

 **Say.**

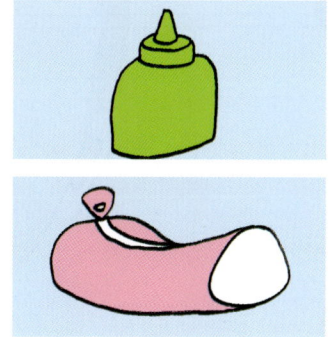

pink   purple   orange

# Unit 2

**6**   **Listen and point. Write the numbers.**

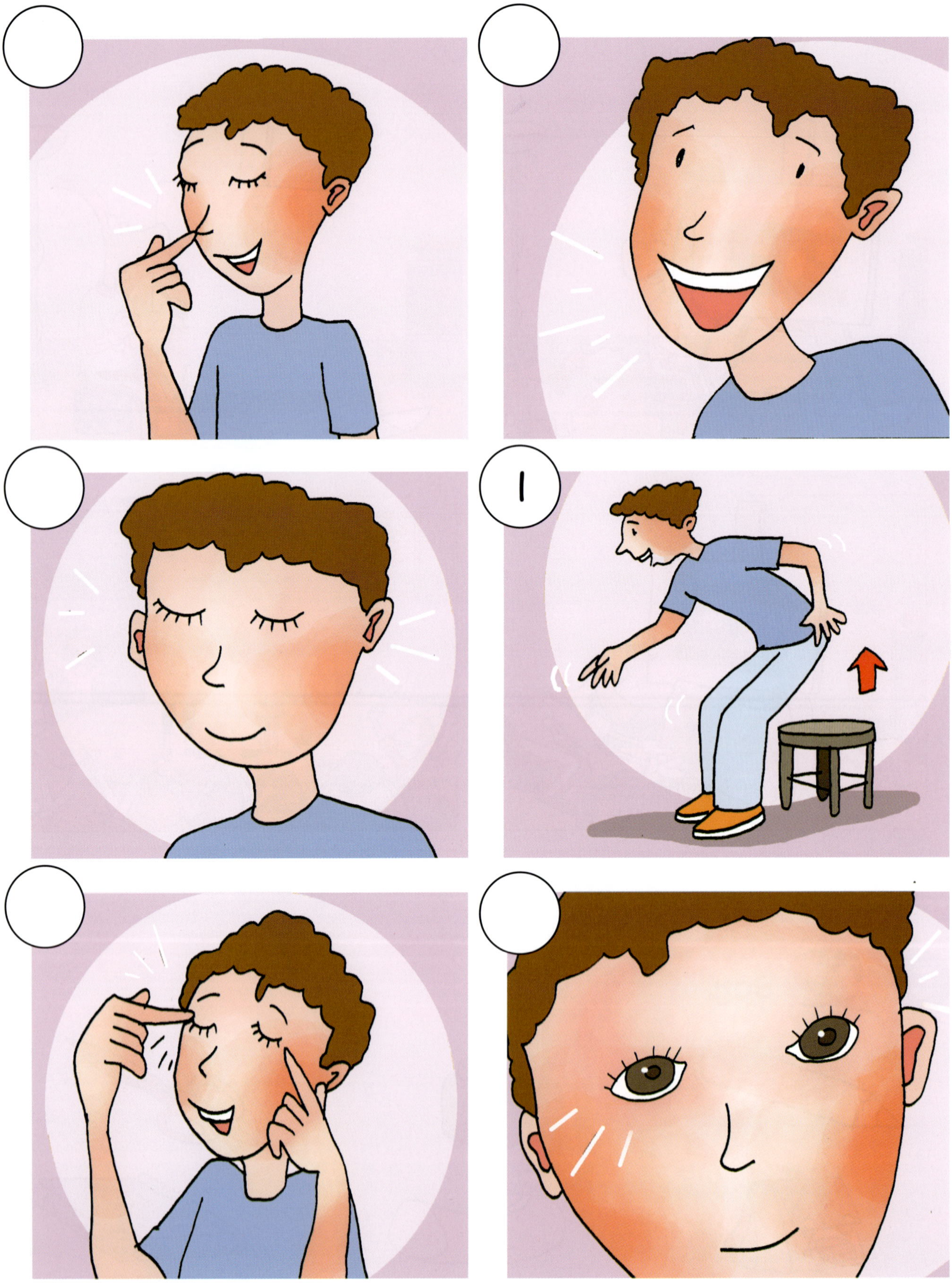

five   six   Close your eyes.   Touch your nose.   Open your eyes.   Listen.   Smile.

**7** Look and guess. Colour.

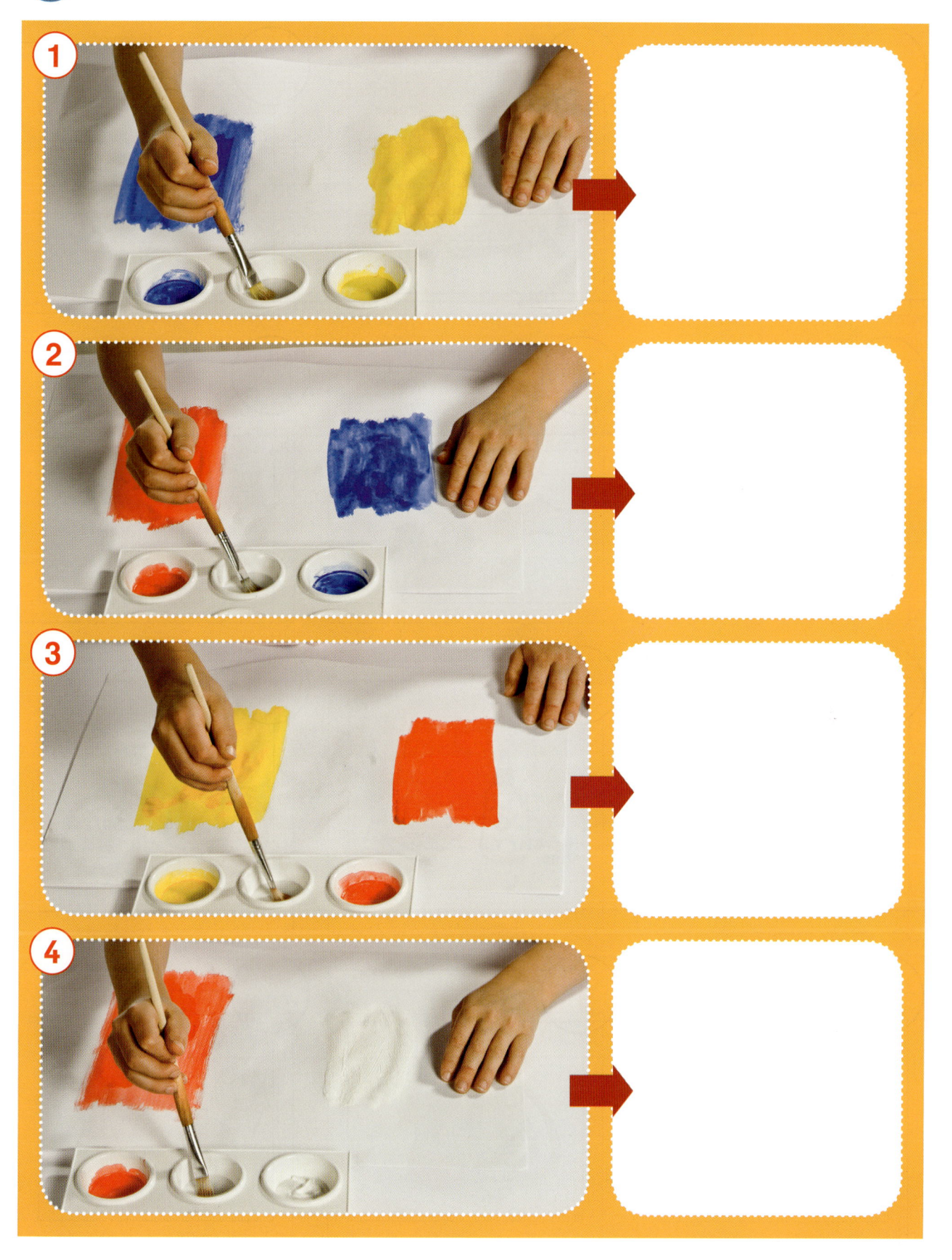

# Units 1-2 — Show what you can do

**1** 🎧 CD 1, 24  Listen and write the numbers. Say and colour.

1

Units
1-2

**2**  **Listen and write the numbers. Say and colour.**

# Unit 3 Fruit

**1**  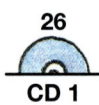  Listen and point.

**2**    Listen. Say and draw.

apple   banana   plum   pear     (Two) apples/bananas/plums/pears.

18

# Unit 3

**3**  **Listen and point. Say the chant.**

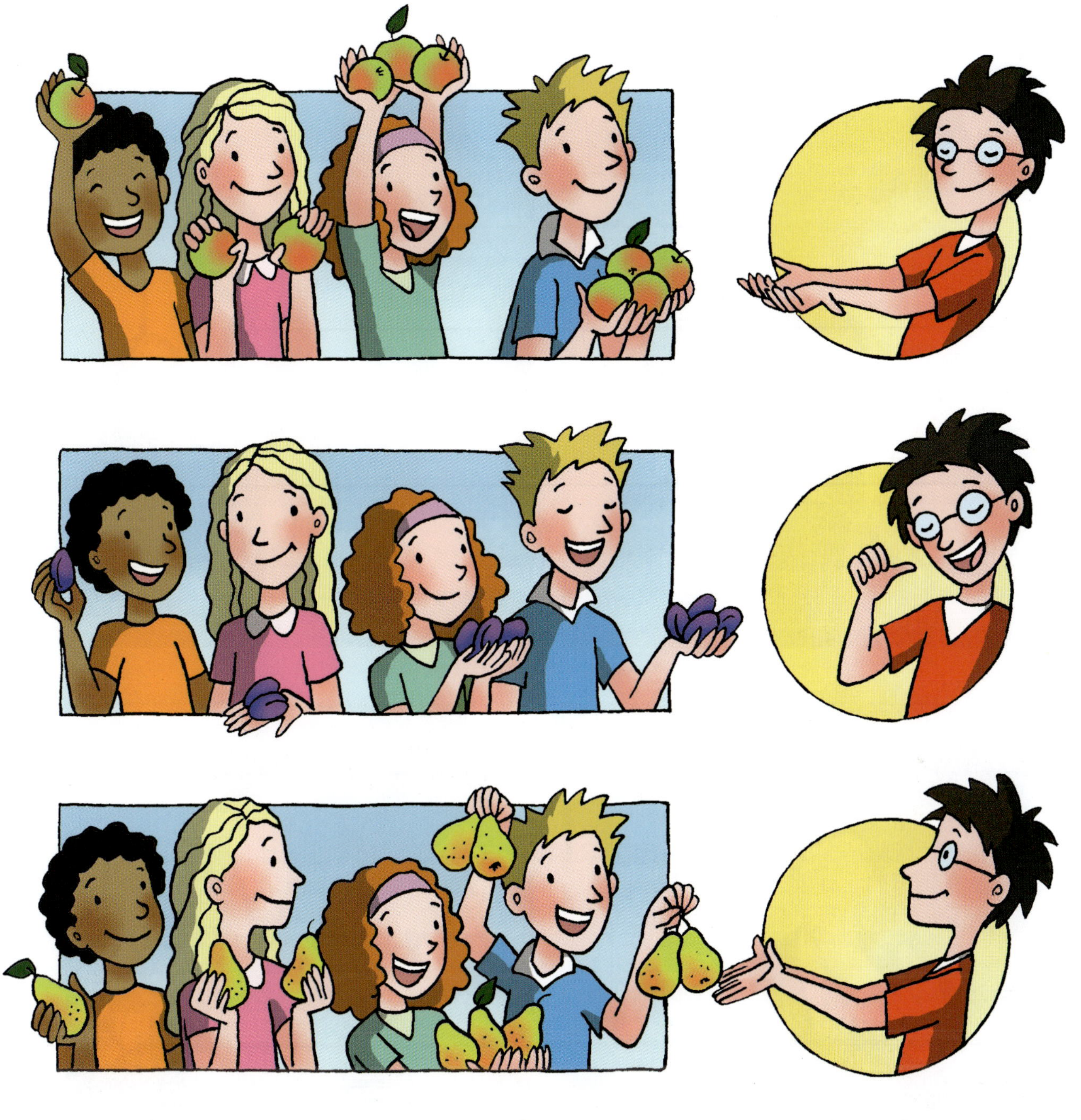

Give me more!   No way!

# Unit 3

**4**   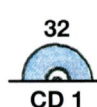 Watch the story. Listen and write the numbers.

**5** 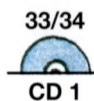 Sing the song.

## 6 Listen and point. Write the numbers.

36 CD 1

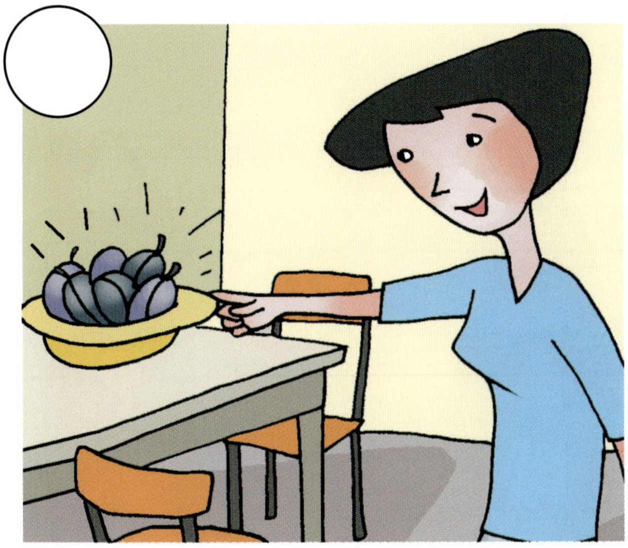

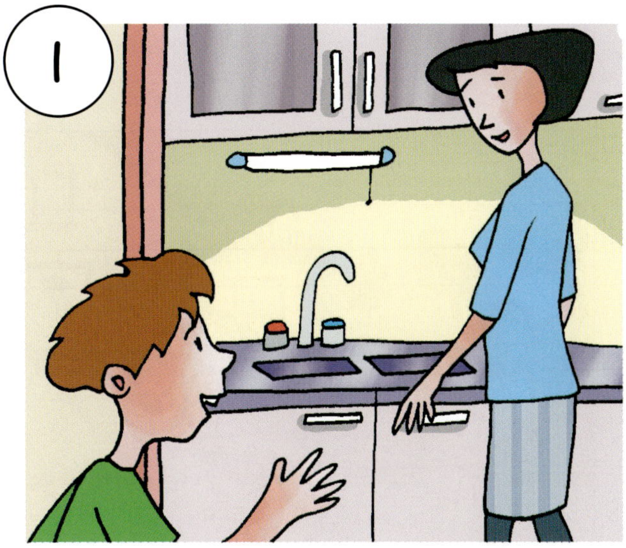


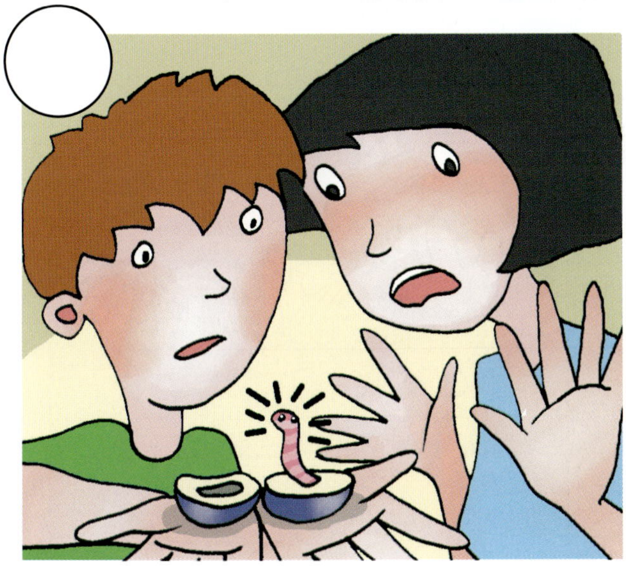

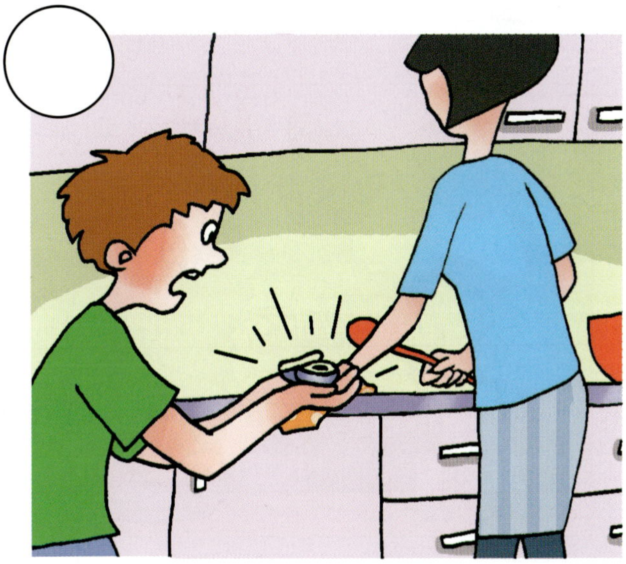

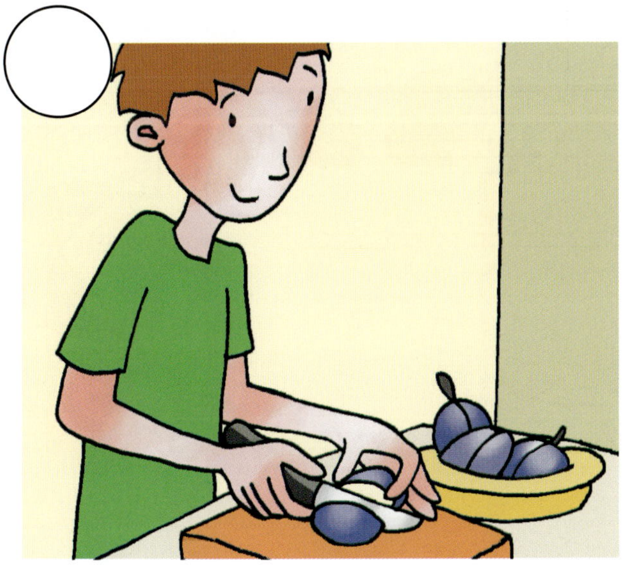

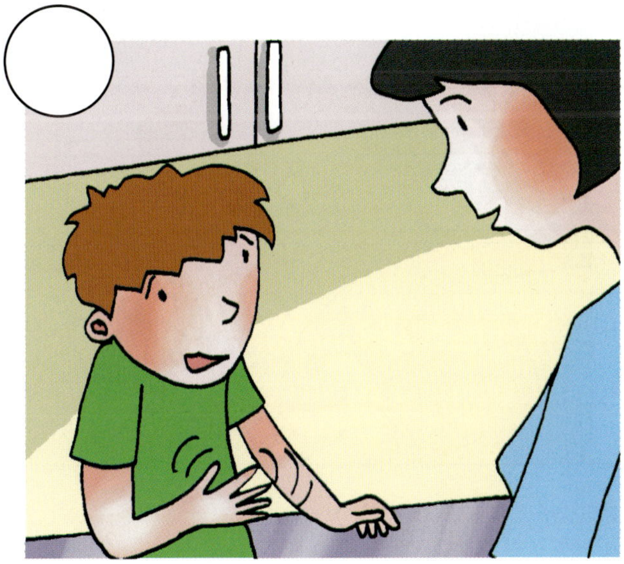

Say 'Hello!' to your mum. You're hungry. Your mum shows you some plums. Cut open a plum.
Show the plum to your mum. Your mum says 'Eek!'.

# Unit 3

**7**   Watch the story. Listen and stick.

I'm thirsty.   I'm hungry.   Help!   Just a moment.

Unit 3

23

# Unit 4 Pets

**1**  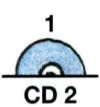 Listen and point. Then say and point.

**2** Think and draw.

cat   dog   hamster   mouse   duck   rabbit

**3**  **Listen and write the numbers. Say the chant.**

What's this?

# Unit 4

**4**   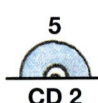 **Watch the story. Listen and stick.**

Let's play.   No, go away!   The mouse is (very) sad.   Let's go to the show.

# Unit 4

# Unit 4

**5**   **Listen and write the numbers.**

1

**6** Make a fishbowl.

Units 3-4

# Show what you can do

**1** 🔊 CD 2 · 10  Listen and write the numbers. Say and colour.

**2** 11 CD 2 **Listen and write the numbers. Say and colour.**

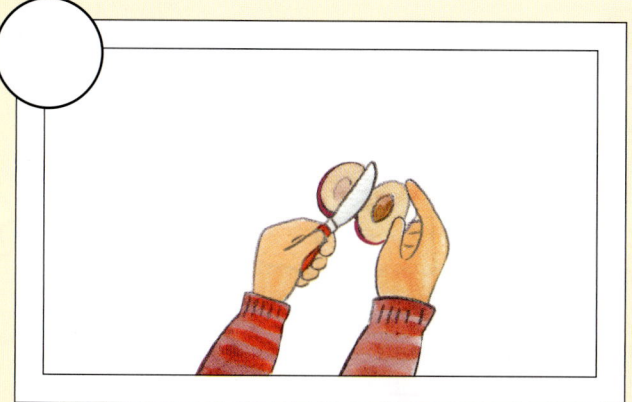

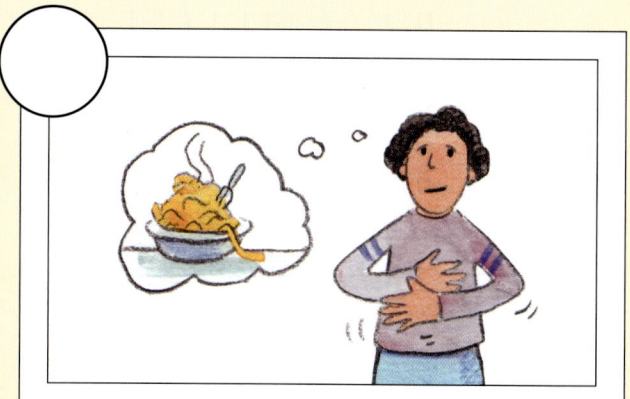

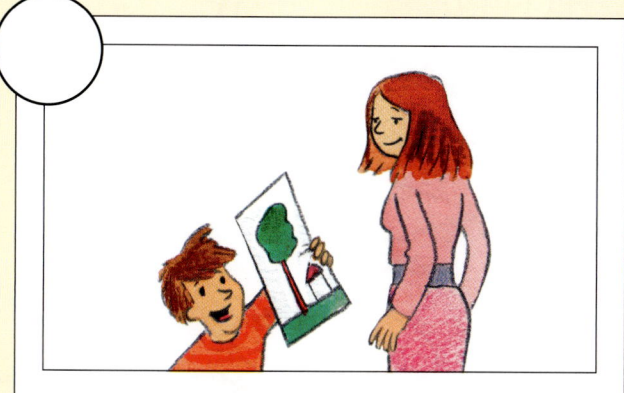

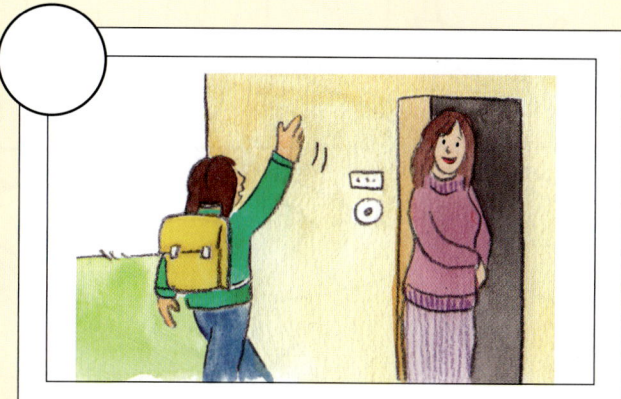

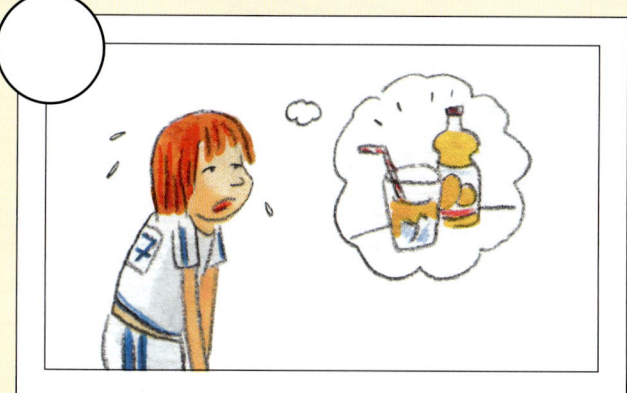

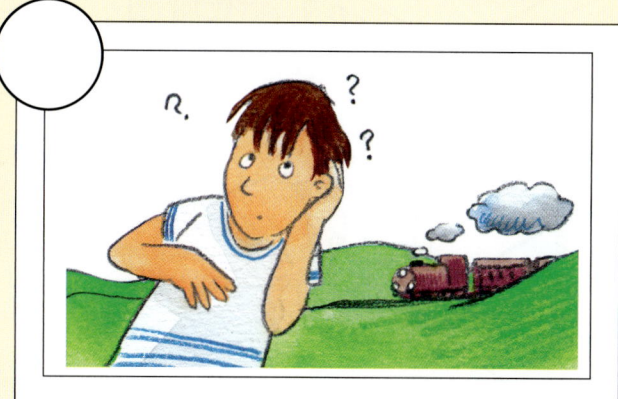

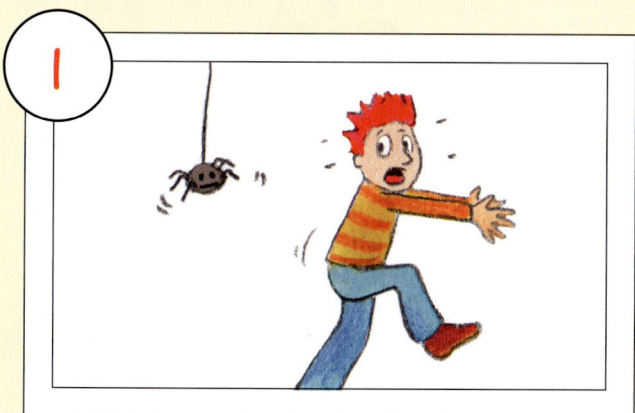

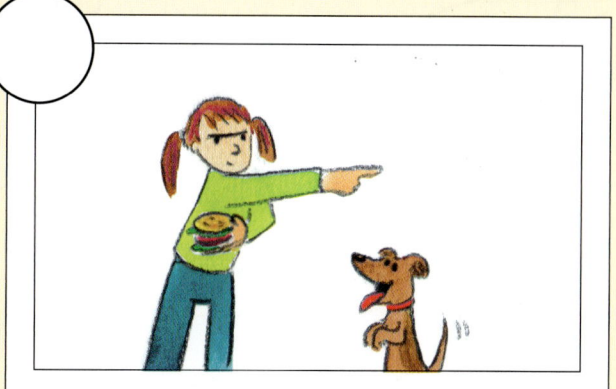

# Unit 5 — Toys

**1** Look and count. Say.

teddy bear   train   plane   car   doll   computer game   ball   puzzle

32

## 2 12/13 CD 2 Listen and point. Say the chant.

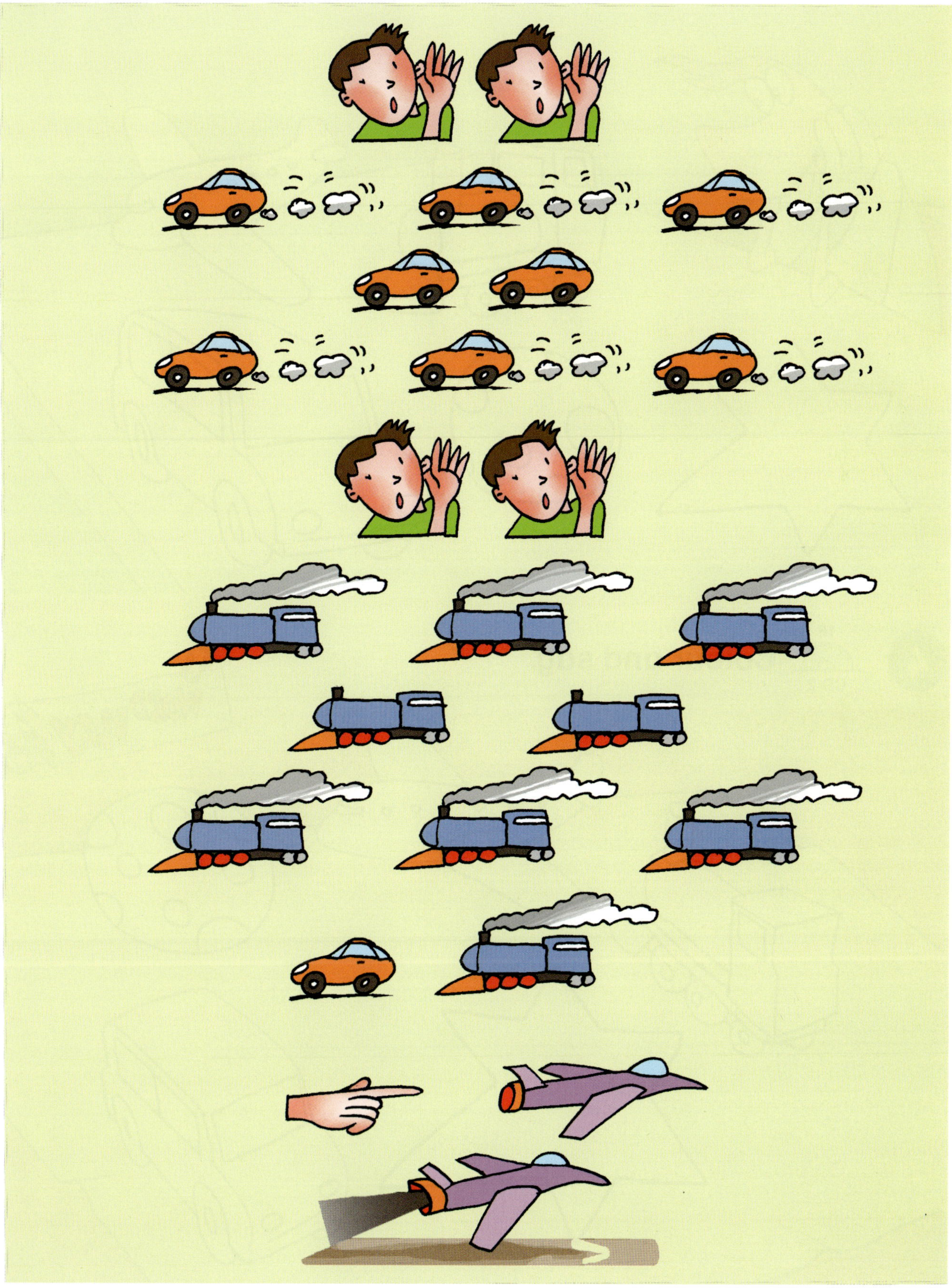

Listen!

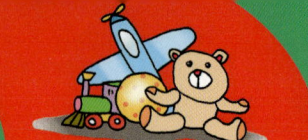

## 3 Listen and colour. Say.

15/16 CD 2

## 4 Colour and say.

16 CD 2

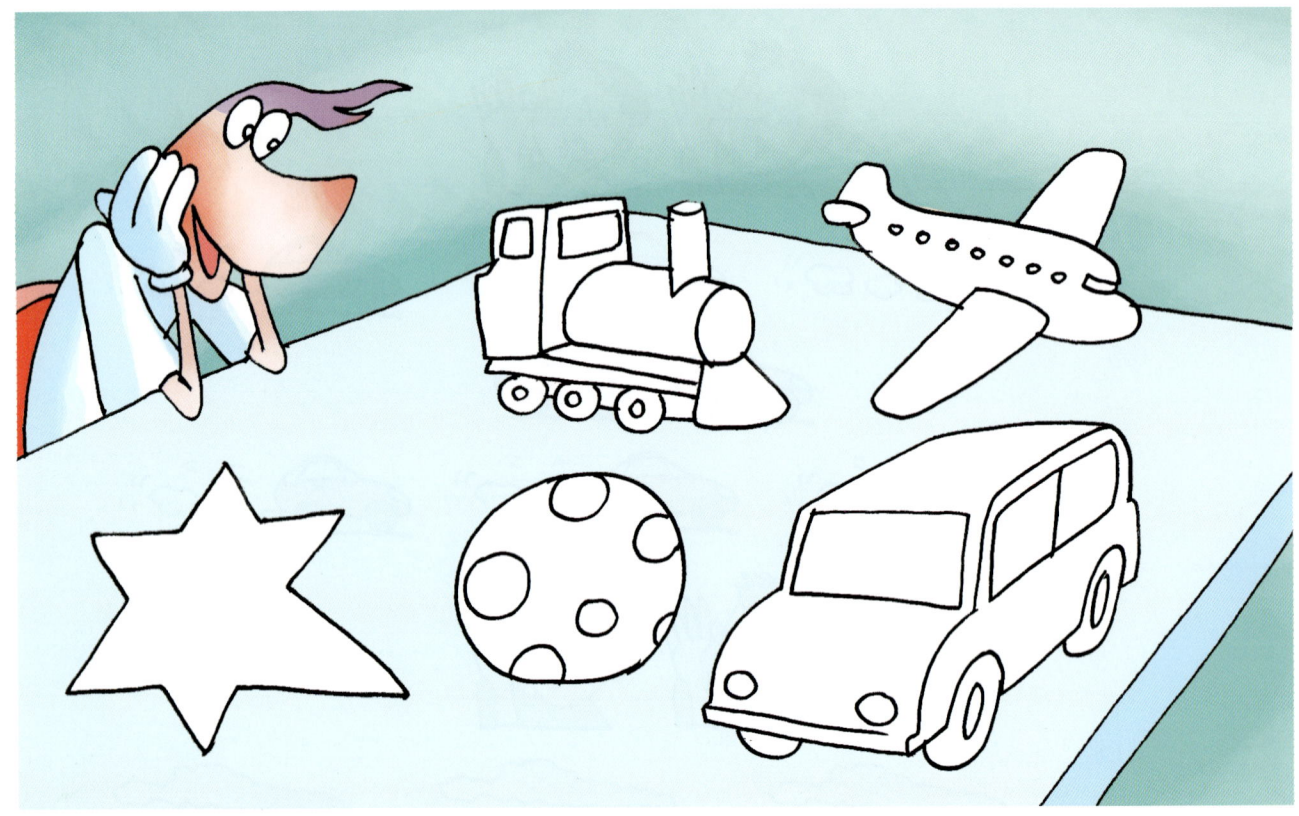

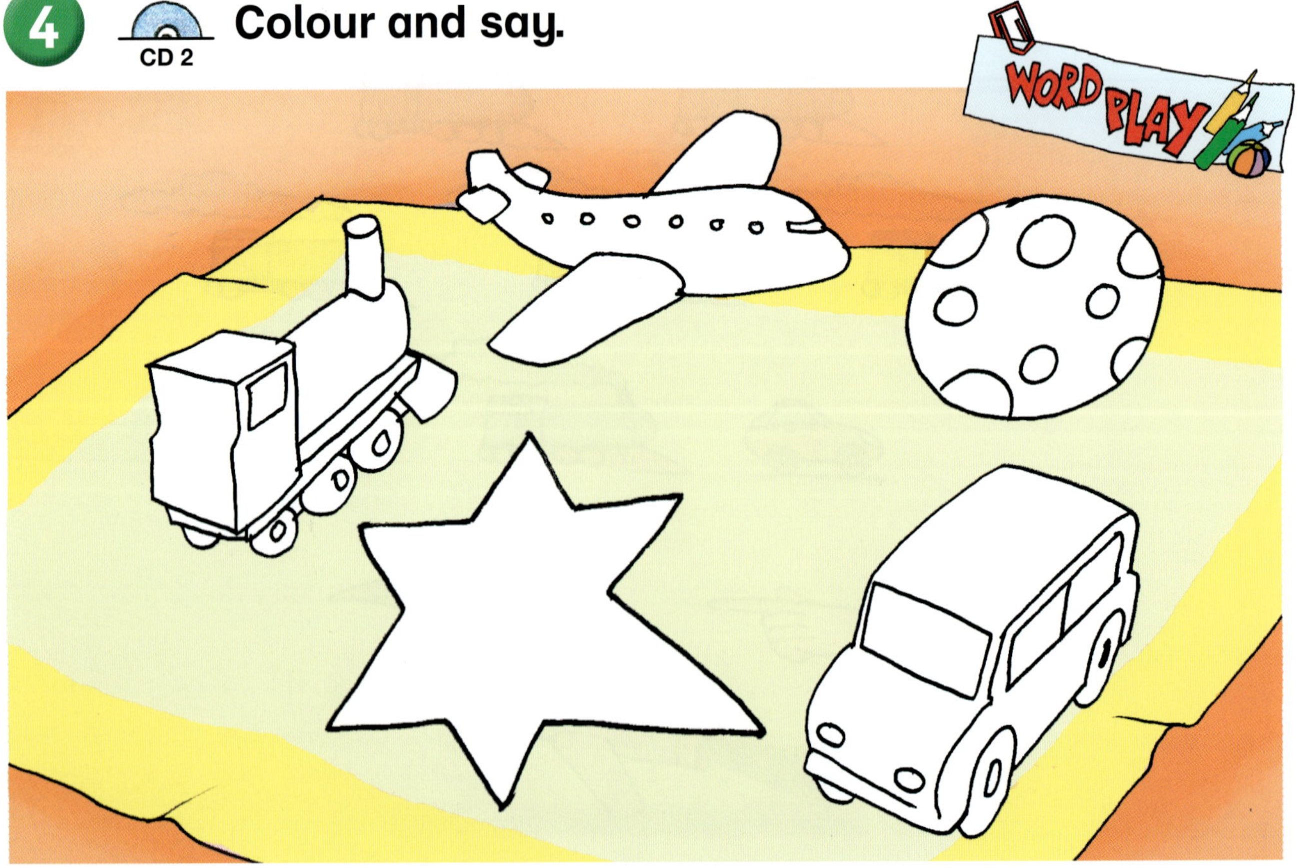


My (blue) (train).   star

**5**  **Listen and point. Write the numbers.**

You're in a car.   There's a (dog).   Stop the car and get out.   The dog jumps into your car.   The dog drives off.
You run after the car.

**35**

# Unit 5

**6**   **Listen and point. Sing the song.**

Unit 5

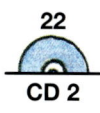

**7** Listen and write the numbers. Draw, write the numbers and say.

|  | Anna | Tom | Lisa |  |
|---|---|---|---|---|
| 🚗 | 2 |  |  |  |
| ✈️ |  |  |  |  |
| 🚆 | 1 |  |  |  |
| 🪆 | 6 |  |  |  |
| 🟠 |  |  |  |  |

**8** Say.

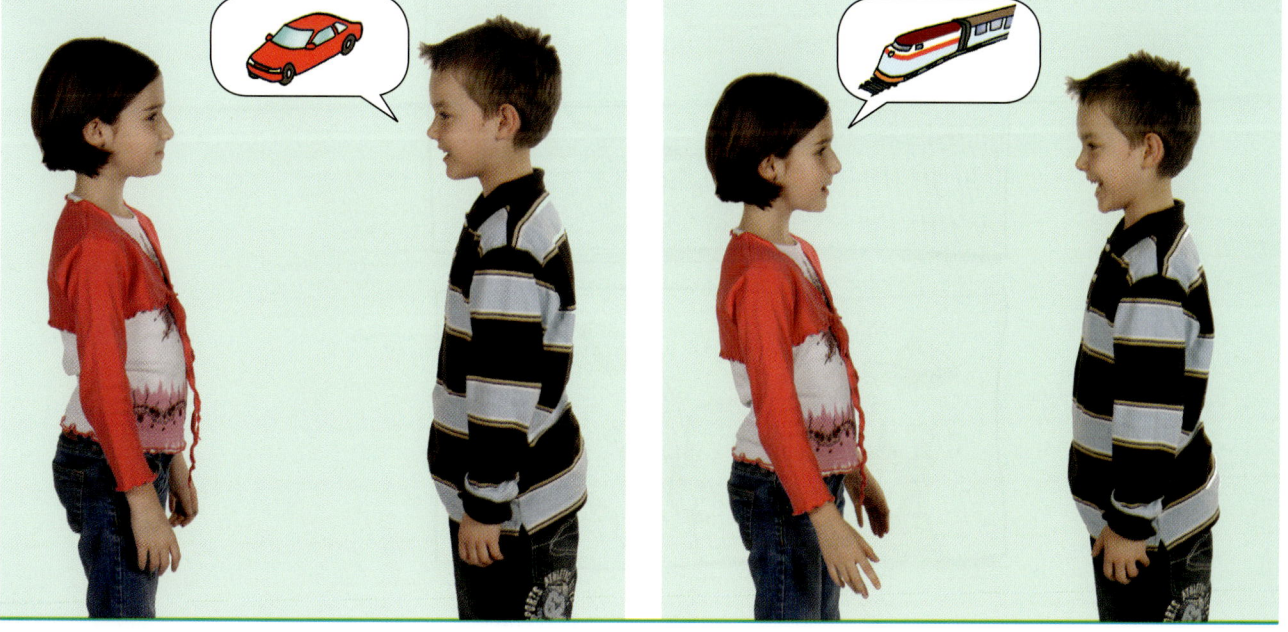

I've got (one) (car).

37

# Unit 6 Weather

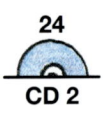

**1** 🎧 CD 2 · 24  Listen and point.

**2** 🎧 CD 2 · 25/26  Listen and point. Say the chant.

rain  sun  wind  clouds  snow   It's raining/snowing/sunny/windy/cloudy.   A cap on a (frog).

38

Unit 6

**3** 🎧 27/28 CD 2 **Listen and point. Say.**

**4** **Look and write the numbers. Say.**

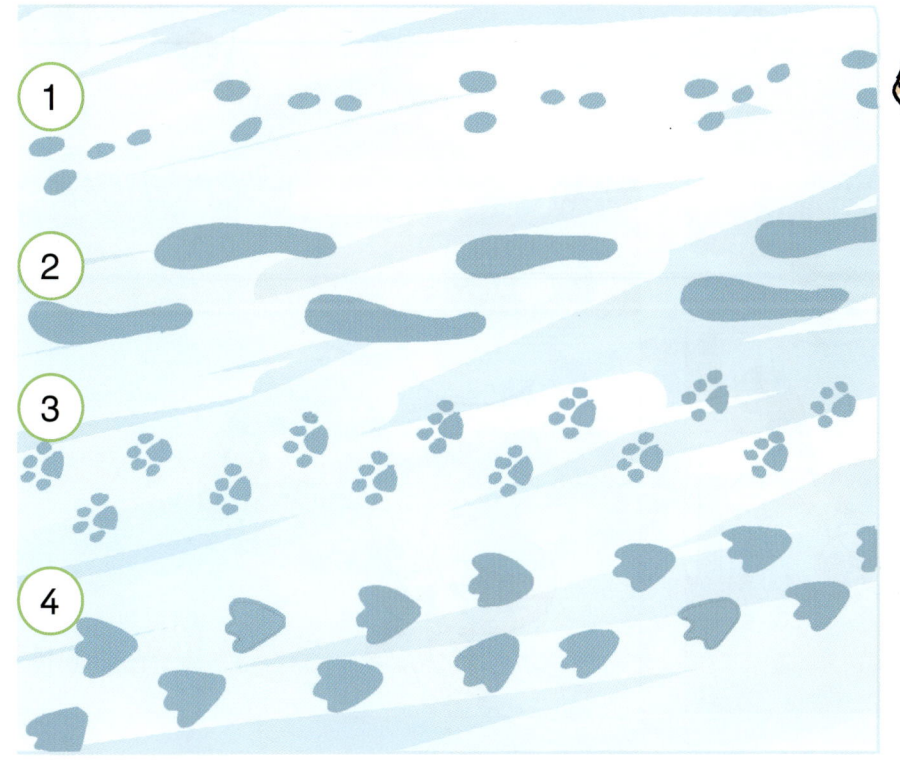

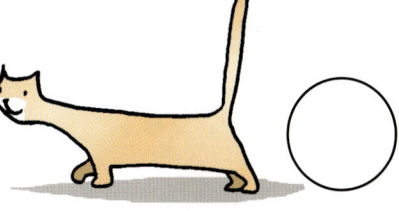

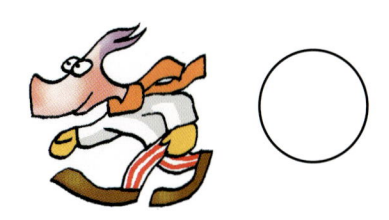

1
2
3
4

1

snowman   grow   run

39

# Unit 6

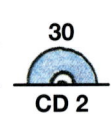

**5** Watch the story. Listen and stick.

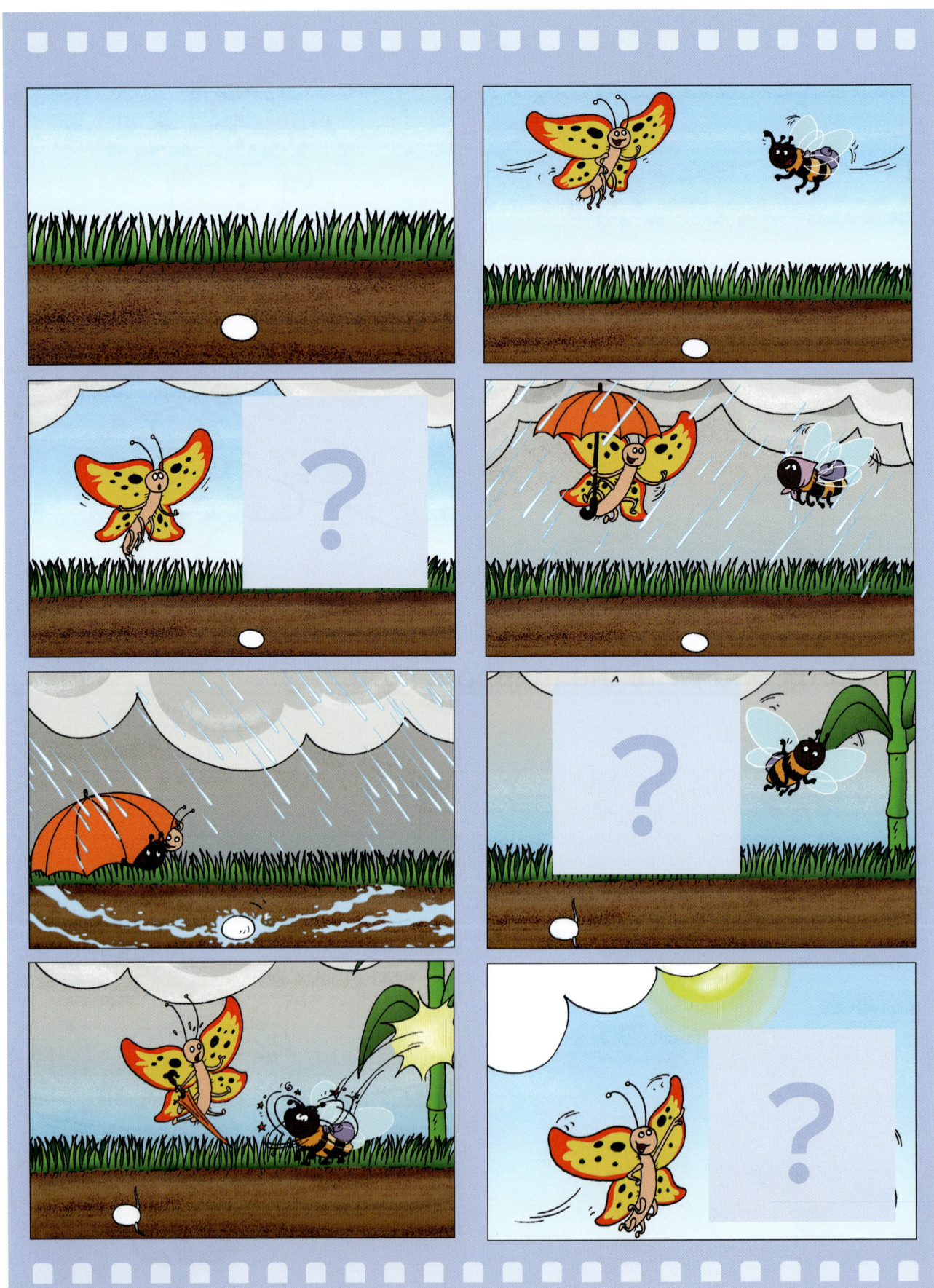

bee   butterfly   a little seed   flower   What a sweet smell!

Unit 6

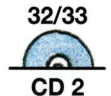

**6** Listen and point. Sing the song.

41

# Unit 6

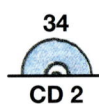

**7** Listen and point. Write the numbers.

( ) ( )

( 1 ) ( )

**8** Say.

**9** Look and colour.

Units 5-6

# Show what you can do

**1** 🎧 CD 2, 37  Listen and write the numbers. Say and colour.

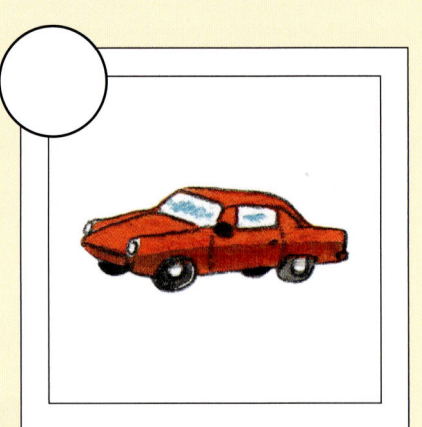

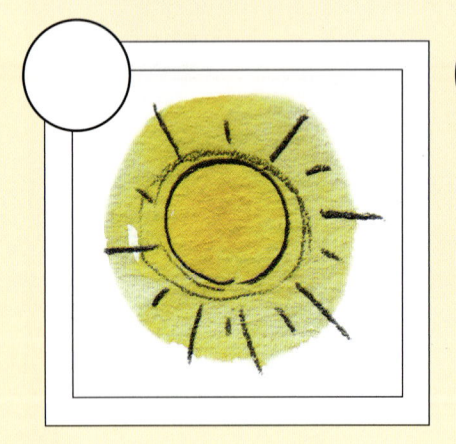

Units 5-6

**2** 🔊 *CD 2 · 38* **Listen and write the numbers. Say and colour.**

1

# Unit 7 Party

**1** Look and count. Say.

sheriff   princess   bear   ghost   clown   frog   monster   nine   ten

Unit 7

**2** Listen and point. Say the chant.

**3** Think and write the numbers.

| 4 | 5 | 6 |
| 8 | 9 | 10 |
| 6 | 7 | 8 |
| 3 |   | 5 |
|   | 2 | 3 |

| 6 | 5 | 4 |
| 8 | 7 | 6 |
| 5 |   | 3 |
| 4 |   | 2 |
|   | 6 | 5 |

A party for a (princess).

47

# Unit 7

**4** 🎧 CD 3 — 5   Listen and point. Write the numbers.

You're a magician.   Get a piece of cake.   A clown grabs your plate.   Turn the clown into a bird.
The bird flies away.   Eat your piece of cake.

**5** 🎧 **Listen and point. Act out.**
CD 3 · 7

What a lovely cake.   Thank you.   Is this your dog?   Yes, it is.   Watch out!   Oh no!

49

# Unit 7

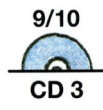

**6** 9/10 CD 3 **Listen and point. Sing the song.**

Unit 7

**7** CD 3 / 10  **Draw and say.**

WORD PLAY

Look at me!   A (ghost) into a (sheriff).

51

# Unit 8 Health

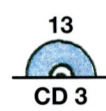

**1** Listen and point. Write the numbers. CD 3 · 13

Get out of bed.   Wash your face.   Clean your teeth.   Bend your knees.   Jump.   Have a glass of milk.

52

Unit 8

**2** Listen and point. Sing the song.

# Unit 8

**3** Watch the story. Listen and write the numbers.

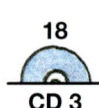

54

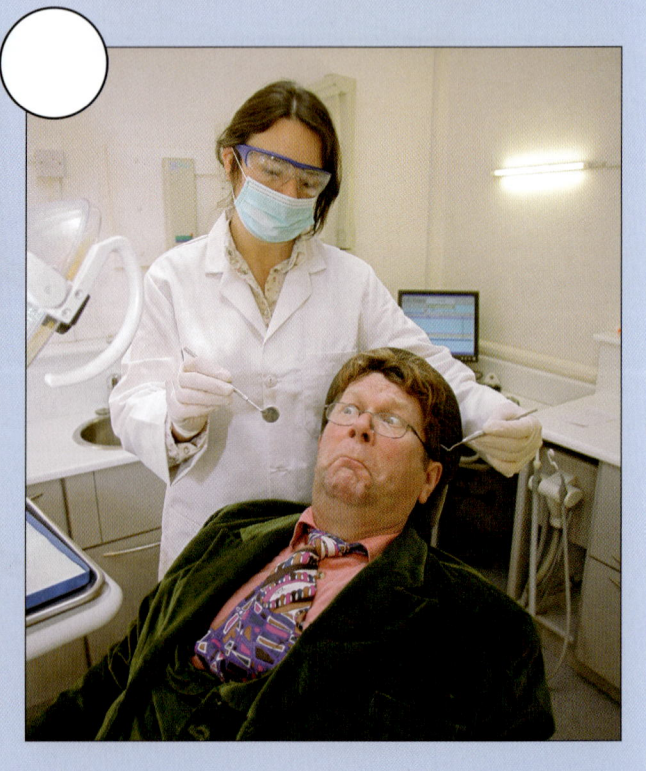

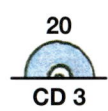

## 4 Listen and point.

(Three) (lollies), please.  Tea's ready.  What's the matter?  I feel sick.

# Unit 8

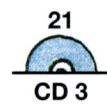

**5** 🎵 21 CD 3  **Listen and point. Act out.**

Go and clean your teeth.   Let's sing a song.

56

Unit 8

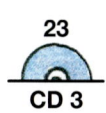

**6** 🎧 CD 3 · 23  **Listen and write the numbers.**

1

Units **7-8**

# Show what you can do

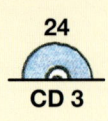

**1** 🎧 **Listen and write the numbers. Say and colour.**
CD 3 24

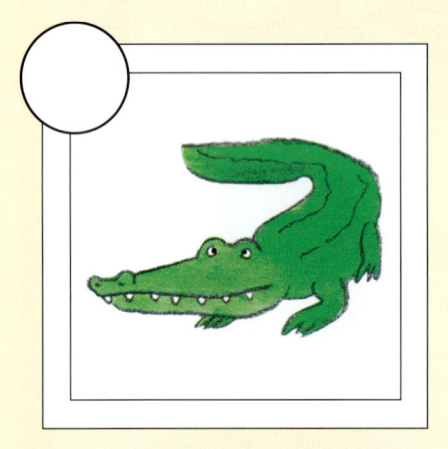

Units 7-8

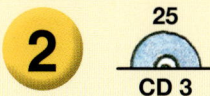

**2** Listen and write the numbers. Say and colour.

# Unit 9 Food

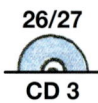

**1** Listen and point. Say the chant.

butter   spaghetti   (Chicken) is great!   cheese   chips   ketchup   Lots of (spaghetti).

Unit 9

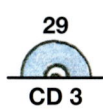

**2** 🔊 29 CD 3 **Listen and colour. Say.**

I like (chips).   cornflakes   milk   pizza

61

Unit 9

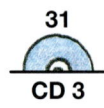

**3** 🎧 CD 3 · 31   **Listen and point. Write the numbers.**

spider   kitchen

62

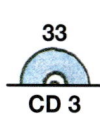

**4** Watch the story. Listen and write the numbers.

# Unit 9

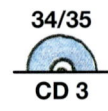

**5** 34/35 CD 3 **Listen and point. Say the chant.**

64

Unit 9

**6** CD 3 / 35  **Draw and say.**

WORD PLAY

# Unit 10 Animals

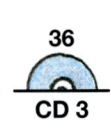

**1** Watch the story. Listen and stick.

lion   elephant   monkey   snake   hippo   The lion is ill.   Listen to my music.   Stop it, please.

Unit 10

# Unit 10

**2** Listen and point. Sing the song.

1, 2, 3

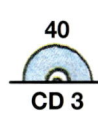

**3** 🖥️ DVD  💿 40 CD 3  **Watch the story. Listen and write the numbers.**

Unit **10**

Unit 10

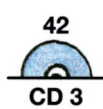

**4** Listen and point. Write the numbers.

1

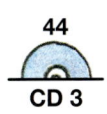

**5** 🎧 **Who lays eggs? Tick the correct pictures (✓). Listen and check.**
CD 3

1. ✓
2. ☐
3. ☐
4. ☐
5. ☐
6. ☐
7. ☐
8. ☐

turtle   whale   mice   penguin

71

**Units 9-10**

# Show what you can do

**1** 🎧 *CD 3, 45* Listen and write the numbers. Say and colour.

Units 9-10

**2** 🔊 46 CD 3  **Listen and write the numbers. Say and colour.**

1

# Picture Dictionary

**Unit 1 Hello**

one  two  three  four  red  yellow  green  blue  black  white  brown  bike  boat  Sit down.  Stand up.  Shout!

**Unit 2 School**

schoolbag  pencil  pencil case  scissors  glue  book  orange  pink  purple  five  six

Unit 3
Fruit

apple   banana   plum   pear   I'm hungry.   I'm thirsty.

Unit 4
Pets

cat   dog   hamster   mouse   duck   rabbit   Go away!   Run!   Kick the ball!

75

## Unit 5 Toys

teddy bear   train   plane   car   doll   computer game   ball   puzzle   star   seven   eight

## Unit 6 Weather

rain   sun   wind   cloud(s)   snow   cap   frog   snowman   flower   umbrella   bee   butterfly   seed

Unit 7
Party

sheriff   princess   bear   ghost   clown   monster(s)   nine   ten   cake   plate   bird   magician   crocodile   prince

77

Unit 8
Health

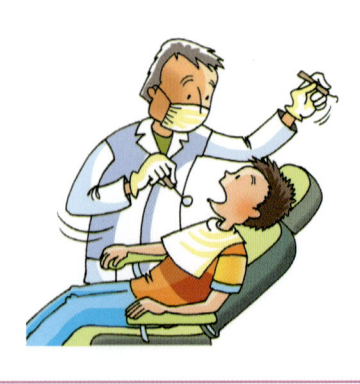

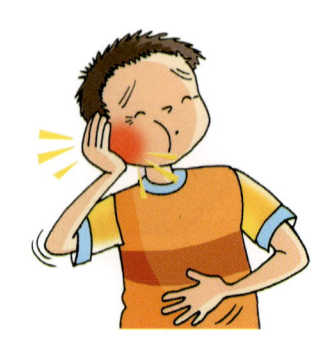

Get out of bed.   Wash your face.   Clean your teeth.   Bend your knees.  Jump.   orange   chocolate   ice cream   milk
Open your mouth.   My tooth hurts.

78

## Unit 9 Food

cornflakes   butter   spaghetti   chicken   spider   eggs   ketchup   chips   pizza   cheese   toast

## Unit 10 Animals

lion   elephant   monkey   snake   hippo

79

**Acknowledgements:**

**The authors and publishers would like to thank the following for permission to reproduce photographs:**
Alamy pp 42 (tlc/wind); 42 (trc/rain); 42 (brc/sun); Stephen Bond pp 29 (fishbowl experiment), 43 (rainbow experiment); Eichholzer Gerda pp 7 (b/children), 15 (painting), 37 (b/children), 42 (b/children); Fotoliaphoto pp 57 (trcr/lunch/Monkey Business), 57 (blcr/hands/Tatyana Gladskih), 71 (tl/turtles/bohanka), 71 (bl/penguins/Bernhard Breton); iStockphoto pp 42 (blc/clouds/Kevin Evans), 57 (tlc/sweets/Stephen Walls, Lisa Marzano, Emre ARICAN, Thomas Perkins), 57 (trcl/tap/Elena Elisseeva), 57 (ml/toothbrush/Adrian Hughes), 57 (mr/apple/Chris Fertnig), 57 (blcl/toilet/Oksana Struk), 57 (brc/running/Jacek Chabraszewski), 71 (tr/whales/Evgeniya Lazareva), 71 (ml/hippos/Peter Malsbury), 71 (mr/snakes/Scott Garrett), 71 (ml/rabbits/ kaphoto), 71 (mr/mice/ Floris Sloof), 71 (br/crocodiles/quesaquo); Charlotte Macpherson Photography pp 20 (Mr Matt), 54 (Mr Matt), 63 (Mr Matt), 69 (Mr Matt)

**The authors and publishers are grateful to the following illustrators:**
Svjetlan Junaković, Zagreb; Mercè Orti, Barcelona; Antje Hagemann, Berlin;
Michael Hülse, Hamburg; Axel Nicolai, Brauweiler

**The publishers are grateful to the following contributors:**
Stephen Bond; Charlotte Macpherson: commissioned photography
Andrew Oliver: cover design
Amanda Hockin: concept design
Hansjörg Magerle – Studio HM: book design and page make-up
Bill Ledger: cover illustration

**Unit 1 Hello**

1

**Unit 2 School**

3

4

**Unit 3 Fruit**

7

## Unit 4 — Pets

## Unit 6 — Weather

## Unit 10 — Animals

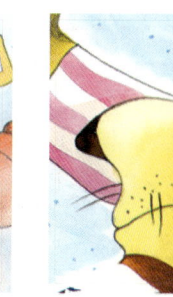